3/97

TOYING AROUND
WITH SCIENCE

TOYING AROUND
WITH SCIENCE

The Physics Behind Toys and Gags

by BOB FRIEDHOFFER

Illustrated by Linda Eisenberg

FRANKLIN WATTS
New York Chicago London Toronto Sydney

To my good friend Dick Wactler

Library of Congress Cataloging-in-Publication Data

Friedhoffer, Robert.
    Toying around with science : the physics behind toys and
    gags / by Bob Friedhoffer ; illustrated by Linda Eisenberg.
        p. cm.
    Includes bibliographical references and index.
    ISBN 0-531-11215-2. — ISBN 0-531-15743-1 (pbk.)
    1. Physics—Study and teaching—Juvenile literature.
2. Toys—Study and teaching—Juvenile literature. 3.
Educational toys—Juvenile literature. [1. Physics. 2. Scientific
recreations. 3. Toys.] I. Eisenberg, Linda, ill. II. Title
QC39.5.F75 1995
688.7'28—dc20   94-49444
                                CIP AC

ACKNOWLEDGMENTS

I would like to thank the following manufacturers, who were kind enough to provide samples and/or information:

Smethport Specialties,
    manufacturer of Wooly Willy®
Larami Corporation,
    manufacturer of the Super Soaker®
Sansom Inc.,
    manufacturer of Crazy Glasses®
Duncan Yo-Yo Company

also:
René Descartes
Mr. Ed
and Annette,
    who let me play with all of the toys at home.

CONTENTS

TOYING AROUND
WITH SCIENCE

INTRODUCTION
WHAT'S A TOY? HAVE YOU EVER REALLY THOUGHT ABOUT TOYS?

When we were small children we played with toys without giving any thought to how they worked. As a matter of fact, most of the toys didn't "work," simply because they were stuffed animals. All that mattered was whether a toy was fun to play with. If it wasn't, we usually put it down and forgot about it.

As we grew a bit older, most of us had at least one kind of mechanical toy. The only thing we knew about that toy was that if we didn't wind the key or change the battery, it wouldn't work. When it didn't work, the toy was quickly placed at the bottom of the toy box or the back of the closet.

As we got older, we didn't want to play with toys, because we thought, *Only babies play with toys*. We still had them; only now they weren't called toys. They were called model planes, erector sets, trains, little homemaker baking ovens, kites, bikes, yo-yos, skateboards, and all sorts of other cool "grown-up" names.

When I got to be about 9 or 10 years old, I wanted to

know what made toys work—the *what if* and the *how come* of toys. I'd take them apart and put them back together again. Sometimes I'd even manage to reassemble them without any parts left over.

I wrote this book so that kids with the same curiosity will have fun playing with toys and learning about what makes them work. I don't want to scare you away, but at the same time you're learning the innermost secrets of toys, you'll also be learning certain scientific principles. As you read through this book, you'll find that science doesn't have to be boring. Amazingly enough, it can actually be fun.

I purposely chose inexpensive toys so that you can buy them and take them apart. At the time this book was written, many items could be bought in 99-cent stores, or variety stores, around the country. If some of the toys are not available in stores in your hometown, close substitutes should be readily available.

I have included some toys that might at first seem very "babyish." But the average person never stops to figure out how they work. When I saw how they actually operate, I thought, "It is so cool that such simple toys operate on scientific principles!" You'll find that many toys use a number of different scientific principles to accomplish their goal of entertaining the user.

The few toy manufacturers mentioned in the book have not paid me in any way to include their products. I chose those toys simply because they are fun and teach an interesting principle.

The toys are organized into broad groupings according to the major scientific principle on which they operate. The back of the book contains a review of the scientific principles discussed in the book and a glossary of words italicized in the text.

Have fun with the toys. Enjoy the book. Next time you're playing with them and your mom tells you to do your schoolwork, you can honestly say, "I *am* doing some work for school. I'm studying science!"

AIR AND WATER PRESSURE TOYS

THE CRAZY GLASSES DRINKING STRAW

The Crazy Glasses® straw may or may not be a toy, but it sure makes drinking a glass of milk—or whatever else you want to drink—a lively experience. It is also a good way to learn about how *air pressure* works.

As you can see in Figure 1, the straw is placed on your face like a regular pair of glasses, except that one earpiece goes into your mouth and the other goes into a glass of liquid refreshment. When you suck on the straw, the milk flows up the long piece, around your eyes and ears, and eventually makes its way into your mouth. It's goofy looking and fun.

I've asked many people, kids and adults alike, "How does the liquid end up in your mouth?"

Most of them answer, "When you sip on the straw, it pulls the liquid up the straw and into your mouth." That's a common answer, but that's not exactly what happens.

The straw works because of air pressure. The air surrounding us pushes on everything with a constant

FIGURE 1

pressure that comes from the weight of the atmosphere. This *atmospheric pressure* decreases as you go higher because the amount of atmosphere overhead becomes less and less (see Figure 2). The density of the atmosphere decreases with altitude as well, because air density lessens with decreasing air pressure.

It's hard for most of us to notice atmospheric pressure. Practically all of us were born close to sea level and our bodies are accustomed to this pressure. At sea level, atmospheric pressure is about 14.7 pounds per square inch (10.1 newtons per square centimeter), or

FIGURE 2

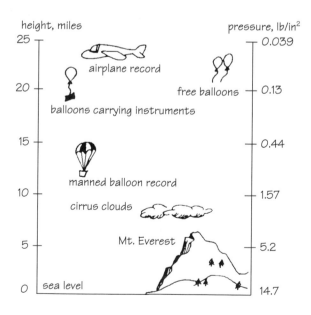

psi. That means that air is pushing downward, upward, and in all directions with a *force* of 14.7 pounds on every square inch of surface that it comes up against.

One place you might notice atmospheric pressure is in the elevator of a tall building. The higher you go in the building the more pressure you feel inside your ears, until you swallow.

Here's why. As you take an elevator up from sea level, air pressure in the elevator decreases. Air pushes on the outside of your eardrum with less force, but air on the inside of the eardrum can still be at atmospheric pressure if the passageway between your throat and ears is blocked with mucus. The higher pressure inside can push on your eardrum, causing discomfort and pain. When you swallow, you clear the blockage, and the pressures equalize—the inside pressure lowers to the same level as the outside pressure.

And now, back to our scheduled program—Crazy Glasses.

When you first place the soda straw into your mouth, the pressures inside your mouth and inside the straw are the same as the pressure pushing down on the surface of the liquid in the glass. They are all at atmospheric pressure—14.7 psi. But when you sip on the straw, you remove air from the space inside your mouth and the straw, so the pressure in that space lowers.

Because the pressure on the liquid's surface is now greater than the pressure in the straw, the liquid rises up the straw, around your ears and eyes, and into your mouth (see Figure 3). Eventually, the pressure inside your

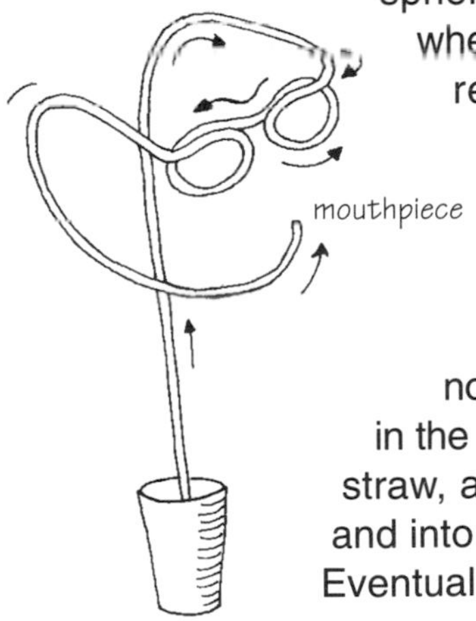

FIGURE 3

mouthpiece

mouth rises back to atmospheric pressure. Then the liquid in the lower part of the straw drops back into the glass. You have to swallow the liquid that's in your mouth and sip again. Of course if you don't want to drink it, you can let it dribble down your chin, but that's very messy and not recommended.

SUCTION CUP

The suction cup is a simple device usually formed from soft rubber or plastic (see Figure 4). By itself, it isn't a toy, but many toys contain suction cups. For example, a suction cup can often be found on the end of a dart from a dart gun (see p. 72) or on the end of an arrow from a bow and arrow (see p. 71).

The suction cup is included in this section because it depends on air pressure to do its job. A suction cup sticks to flat, *nonporous* (airtight) surfaces, such as the outside of a refrigerator door or a smooth kitchen countertop. When pressed against the surface, the suction cup flattens and the volume inside the cup decreases. Most of the air inside the cup is pushed out around the rim of the cup.

Because the suction cup material is *elastic*, it attempts to return to its original shape, just as a stretched

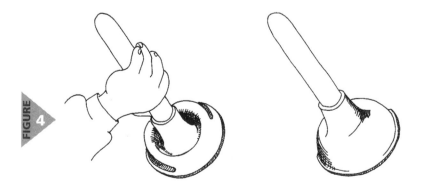

FIGURE 4

18

spring does. To accomplish this, the cup must increase its interior volume. But now there is less air in the cup. Air cannot reenter the cup from the outside because there is a seal between the cup and the surface it is pushing against. And air cannot enter through the cup material or the surface because they are both nonporous.

Air is pushing on the outside surface of the suction cup with atmospheric pressure of 14.7 psi. But as the cup moves back to its original shape, the air pressure inside the cup decreases to less than 14.7 psi because air density is decreasing. Because the air pressure pushing on the outside of the suction cup is greater than the pressure inside the cup, the cup is squeezed tightly against the nonporous surface and is held in place.

THE KETCHUP SQUIRTER

The ketchup squirter is a nifty toy and an awesome gag to have around the kitchen table or backyard barbecue. It's the regular old ketchup-dispensing squeeze bottle that everyone has seen before. With 2 minutes of mod-

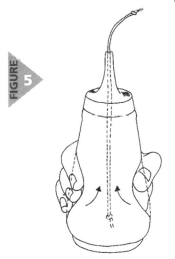

FIGURE 5

ification, it becomes a great practical joke.

First, go to a housewares store and buy a new ketchup squeeze bottle, similar to the one in Figure 5. Or clean up an old one if you have it. Next get about 15 to 20 inches (38 to 51 cm) of red string or yarn that will just fit through the nozzle. It is important that the string fill the hole but slide through fairly easily; otherwise, the toy will not work. With the nozzle off the bottle, pull the string through the hole, and tie a small knot on each end of the string to prevent it from sliding out of the nozzle.

Then pull the string backward through the nozzle until only the knot is left sticking out on top. Put the string inside the bottle and screw on the nozzle.

Pick up the bottle and aim it at someone: then squeeze hard.

NOTE *Don't ever aim toward anyone's face; you could hit someone in the eye and cause an injury.*

Squeezing the bottle increases the pressure inside. Because air is a gas, it compresses into the smaller volume, and the air density increases. As a result, the air pressure inside the bottle becomes greater than atmospheric pressure.

As soon as the pressure in the bottle is great enough, it pushes the string out the nozzle. Air rushes out with the string, and the *friction* between the string and the air also helps drag the string out.

When the person you have aimed at sees this red stuff coming, he or she assumes it's ketchup. This is one cool practical joke that will hurt no one, unless the

person you pull it on doesn't have a sense of humor—
and is a lot bigger than you and can run faster than you.
You have been warned.

THE JUMPING SPIDER

You can usually find the jumping spider toy, or gag,
around Halloween time. It looks like a big old hairy spider with a leash. What you do is set the spider on the
ground or on a tabletop. When somebody bends over
to take a look at it, you make the spider jump—and this
makes the person jump even higher.

The leash is really a plastic tube. One end of the
tube connects to a rubber squeeze bulb that you keep in
your hand. The other end connects to a curled rubber
bladder that's hidden on the underside of the spider
(see Figure 6).

The spider's rubber bladder is elastic, and at normal air pressure, it's all curled up. When curled up, it
takes up very little space under the spider. The squeeze
bulb in your hand is also elastic and is filled with air.

When the bulb is squeezed, the air inside is compressed. As the pressure inside the bulb increases, air

FIGURE 6

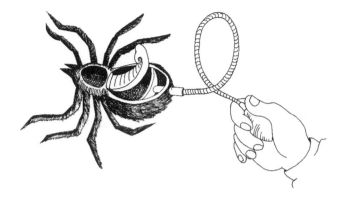

is forced from the bulb. The air travels through the tube and has enough pressure to inflate the rubber bladder. As the bladder rapidly inflates, it pushes sharply against the ground, causing the spider to jump.

When you release your grip on the bulb, both the bulb and the rubber bladder go back to their original shapes because they are elastic. Air flows from the bladder through the tube and back into the rubber bulb.

THE SPUD GUN

The spud gun is an awesome toy that was around back in the "nifty fifties." It's called a spud gun because of its ammunition—the potato, or lowly spud, a member of the deadly nightshade family. This ammunition can be found in all the supermarkets and produce stores across our fair land.

Spud guns show up every now and then but are not always available—so buy one, or two if you can, whenever you see them.

To load the ammunition for this one-shot gun, insert the barrel tip into a potato (see Figure 7). A small chunk of potato should break off and lodge inside the air inlet. The piece of potato blocks air from entering and leaving the cylinder.

The gun consists of an inner barrel that slides inside

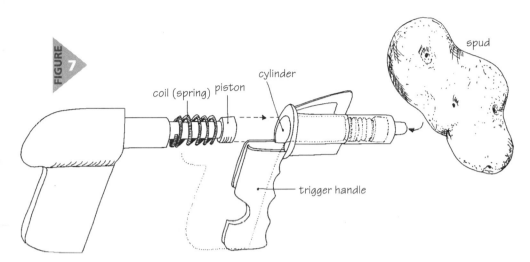

FIGURE 7

spud

cylinder

coil (spring) piston

trigger handle

an outer barrel, the cylinder. The inner barrel has a spring wrapped around it and a piston head on its end. The piston head's outside diameter is just a touch smaller than the inside diameter of the cylinder. To prevent air from escaping around the rim of the piston head, a lubricating sealant much like petroleum jelly is smeared around the outside of the piston.

When you squeeze the trigger, the two barrels slide together. The spring compresses and the cylinder moves over the piston. As the air space inside the cylinder gets smaller, the air in the cylinder compresses. When the air pressure in the space becomes high enough, it forces the potato ammunition in the tip to shoot out.

If you've aimed well, you should hear a satisfying splat as you hit your target.

NOTE *Do not shoot at anyone; you could hit someone in the eye and cause an injury.*

When you release the trigger, the spring returns to its original shape. This pushes the cylinder and piston away from each other, increasing the space inside the cylinder.

As the cylinder enlarges, air flows into the air inlet, setting up "the deadly spud gun" for its next shot.

WATER GUN

Almost everyone has played with a water gun at one time or another. It's probably the perfect outdoor summer toy. If it is well aimed, it can help you and your friends cool off while you're running around in the sun having a good time. This is one toy you can point at others without hurting anyone.

Water guns are actually small water pumps (see Figure 8). The body of the gun acts as a reservoir: it holds the water that squirts out. When you squeeze the trigger, you are actually pushing a piston into a cylinder and, at the same time, compressing a spring inside. Upon release of the trigger, the spring pushes the piston back out of the cylinder.

To begin shooting the gun, you must prime the pump. That means you have to pull back the trigger a few times before water begins pumping. When you pull the trigger back, the piston pushes against the air inside the cylinder. The air cannot escape the cylinder unless one of two *valves* opens. One valve is at the top of the cylinder and the other is at the bottom. They both open only when a force pushes up on them.

When the piston compresses the air inside the cylinder, the increased air pressure pushes down on the lower valve, keeping it closed. But the air presses up on the upper valve, forcing it open and allowing air to flow out of the cylinder into the outlet tube. Once the piston has pushed the air out, gravity pulls the upper valve downward and closes it. As the trigger releases, the spring pushes the piston back out of the cylinder. Because no air can get in to fill the expanding space, the air pressure lowers inside the cylinder.

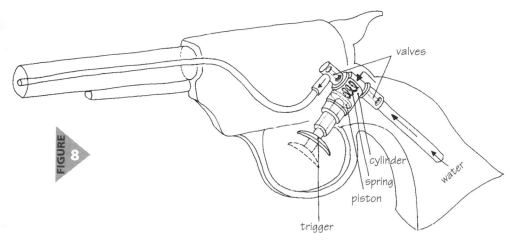

FIGURE 8

valves

cylinder

spring

piston

water

trigger

Because the lowered pressure is less than the atmospheric pressure pushing on the surface of the water in the reservoir, the water rises up the tube (just as it does in the crazy straw) and pushes the lower valve open.

As water flows into the cylinder, the difference in air pressure disappears and gravity pulls the lower valve closed. Now the gun is ready to pump water. When the trigger is pulled again, the water in the cylinder is forced out through the upper valve and into the outlet tube, allowing you to squirt your friends and create havoc.

The total amount of water shot with each pull of the trigger is determined by the size of the cylinder. The distance the water shoots depends on the amount of pressure you build on the water in the cylinder—in other words, the amount of force you use in pulling the trigger.

THE SUPER SOAKER

The Super Soaker® water gun is relatively new. At the time this book was written, it had been around for only three or four years. Compared to a regular water gun, it's darn amazing. It shoots a large quantity of water an astounding distance. Although it is more expensive than most toys in this book, I've included it because it operates on an interesting variation of the regular water gun.

In this toy, the water is not held in the body of the gun but in a tank on top (see Figure 9). The tank is a water-and-compressed-air bottle, which I will call "the bottle" for short. Before you can shoot the gun you must fill the bottle halfway with water. Make sure you fill it only about halfway or the gun won't work properly.

Next, you have to pressurize the bottle by pumping the air pump in and out with your hand. This moves a piston in and out of a cylinder, forcing air through the main air valve. As the air moves into the bottle, air pressure builds in the space above the water. If there is too much water in the bottle, there will not be enough air pressure to push the water out when you shoot the gun.

The pumping of the air is made possible by the main air valve and the air inlet valve. The main air valve opens when air in the cylinder is pumped toward it (the in-stroke), but a spring behind the valve keeps it shut at all other times so air doesn't escape from the bottle. The air inlet valve on the head of the piston (see close-up A in the figure) lets air into the cylinder on the out-stroke of the pump but seals off the cylinder during the in-stroke to prevent air from escaping. On the out-stroke, friction between the cylinder walls and the *O-ring* pulls the O-ring away from the air inlet opening so that air can pass. But during the in-stroke, the O-ring moves back over the air-inlet opening, blocking the passage of air.

When you have pumped the air pressure in the bottle to a high level, you are ready to shoot water. The trigger is actually one end of a lever that, when acti-

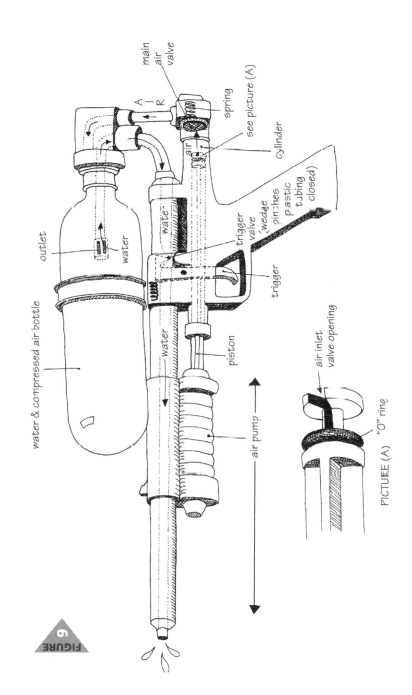

FIGURE 9

water & compressed air bottle

outlet

water

main
air
valve

A
I
R

spring

see picture (A)

air

cylinder

water

trigger
valve
(wedge
pinches
plastic
tubing
closed)

trigger

water

piston

← air pump →

PICTURE (A)

air inlet
valve opening

"O" ring

vated, releases the pressurized water in the bottle out through plastic tubing in the barrel. The other end of the lever, inside the gun, normally holds the water back by pinching the soft tubing closed. The lever is held in place by a rather strong spring.

When you squeeze the trigger, the wedge lifts off the plastic tubing, and the high air pressure in the bottle forces water out the barrel.

MAGNETIC TOYS

WOOLY WILLY

The Wooly Willy® has been around for a long time. I remember it from my childhood. It's an oldie but a goody.

The idea is to move a magnet underneath a cardboard sheet printed with Willy's face on it (see Figure 10). When you move the magnet, you arrange iron filings on his face so that it looks as if he has hair, a beard, a mustache, sideburns, and so on.

The picture of Willy is covered by a plastic bubble that prevents the iron filings from scattering about.

Why are iron filings attracted to the magnet?

Magnets possess a *magnetic field*, a force field that extends into the space around the magnet and attracts certain substances. One of these substances is iron.

Each iron filing on Wooly Willy has many *magnetic domains* within it. Magnetic domains are actually microscopic magnets within a magnetic or magnetizable object. Like all magnets, they have a north and a south pole, which designate the direction of the magnetic field.

FIGURE 10

In nonmagnetized iron filings, the poles of the domains point in many different directions. They're all jumbled up, so that overall, each filing has no noticeable magnetic field.

When a magnet is in the vicinity of the iron filings, the magnetic domains are forced by the field to line up so that their north and south poles point in the same direction as the poles of the big magnet. The iron filings themselves become temporary magnets, resulting in a magnetic force of attraction between them and the big magnet.

You may have heard that opposites attract. That phrase certainly applies to magnets. North poles are attracted to south poles and south poles to north poles.

Similar poles, on the other hand, repel each other. North poles are repelled by north poles and south poles are repelled by south poles.

An easy way to see whether this is true is to get two small bar magnets and place them together. You will find that they stay together when opposite poles are placed next to each other and repel each other when like poles are placed next to each other.

Once the magnetic field is removed from the area of the filings, the domains jumble up once again. That's why they're called temporary magnets. The ability of a magnet to magnetize an adjacent piece of iron is called *magnetic induction.*

THE BUG IN THE MUG

The bug in the mug is a great toy, or practical joke, that uses magnetic attraction. You can make it with simple materials from a hardware store or variety store.

First, you'll need a plastic bug. You'll also need two small round alnico magnets, about 3/8 in (1 cm) in diameter. Alnico is an alloy consisting of aluminum, nickel, and cobalt. (You can also get these from Edmund Scientific, 101 E. Gloucester Pike, Barrington, N.J. 08007-1380.)

NOTE *Do not use any other kind of magnet; certain rare earth magnets can poison you if you touch them and then touch your fingers to your mouth.*

With epoxy glue, attach one of the magnets to the bottom of the bug.

After the glue has set, you're ready to horrify your friends.

Place the bug in a ceramic or plastic mug, keeping the magnet against the mug's wall. Hold the other magnet on the outside of the mug wall as shown in Figure 11. The two magnets should attract each other and stay in place. Fill the mug with enough dark-colored soda to cover the bug.

Concealing the outer magnet in your hand, offer the mug to a friend. But before you release it, look inside the mug and innocently ask, "What's that?" At the same time, secretly move the outer magnet so that the bug starts to slide up the inside of the mug's wall. Your friend will see what looks like a live bug crawling out of the soda. If the bug has done its job, your friend will be quite horrified.

This prank works because the north pole of one magnet is adjacent to the south pole of the other magnet. The poles attract each other even though they are separated by a ceramic or plastic barrier. And the attrac-

tion between them is quite strong, as shown by the fact that the inner magnet actually follows the outer one when you move it with your fingers.

If you follow these instructions, you'll have one cool toy, thanks to magnetism.

FRICTION TOYS

THE LITTLE CLIMBING DUDE

The little climbing dude comes in a variety of shapes and sizes. Through the years, the "dude" has been shaped like a flower, animal, monster, hot air balloon, and so forth. Today the toy is frequently made by hand and can be found in craft stores.

First, you hang the dude from the string on a nail as in Figure 12. Holding a button in each hand, pull the string taut so that the dude hangs straight down. Then alternately pull on the buttons, and the little climbing dude appears to climb up the string. When he reaches the top and you release the buttons, the little guy falls down to the starting position, ready to climb again.

This toy works because of friction and gravity.

As you pull the button on the right as shown in Figure 13, the crossbar tilts down toward the right. The string passes in a straight line through the hole in the arm on the right side.

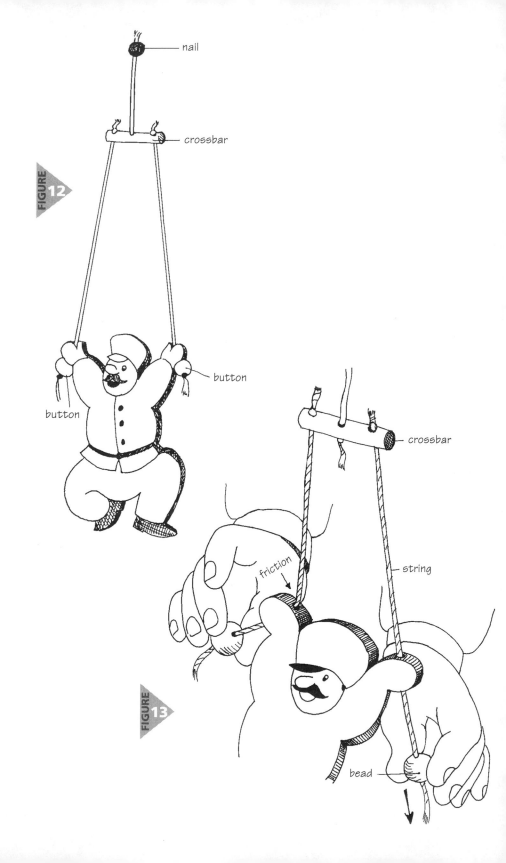

FIGURE 12

nail

crossbar

button

button

FIGURE 13

crossbar

friction

string

bead

But the left arm rises up the string. The string bends as it passes through the hole in the arm, creating a bit of frictional resistance between the string and the arm. As a result, the arm stays in place on the string.

When you pull the second button and relax the first, the resistance changes sides, and the right side rises. Alternately pulling on each side causes it to climb up the string.

When he's at the top and you release the buttons, gravity conquers friction. The little climbing dude falls to the bottom of the strings, where he is stopped by the buttons.

If you don't want to go to the trouble of buying a wooden dude, you can make one with a playing card using Figure 14 as a guide.

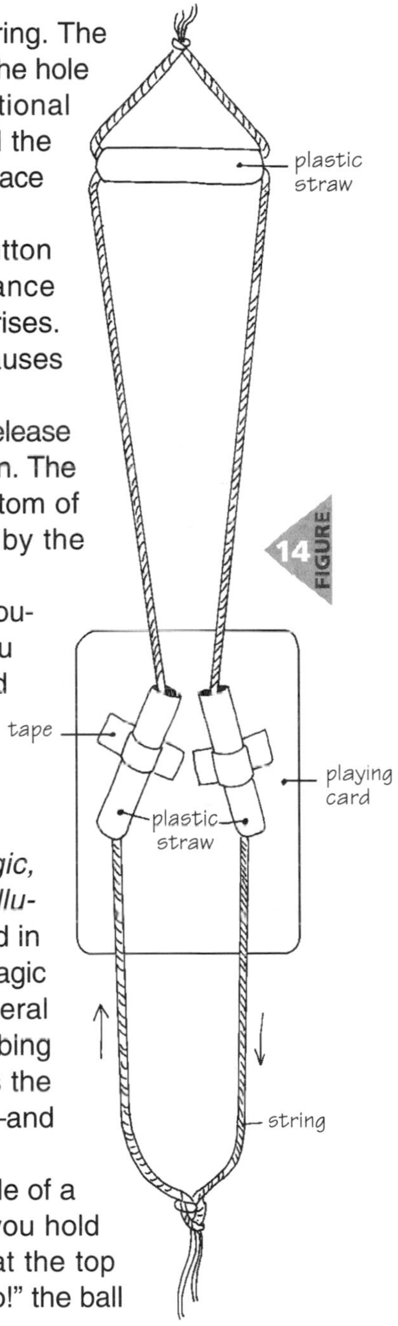

THE MAGIC BALL

In old magic books, such as *Magic, Scientific Diversions and Stage Illusions* by Albert Hopkins, published in 1897, there is a trick called "The Magic Ball" that works on the same general scientific principle as the little climbing dude. In this case, friction causes the ball to remain static—to stay still—and gravity causes it to move.

A string runs through the middle of a wooden ball. Using both hands, you hold the string vertically with the ball at the top of the string. On the command "Go!" the ball

FIGURE 14

plastic straw

tape

playing card

plastic straw

string

FIGURE 15

drops, and on the command "Stop!" the ball comes mysteriously to a halt.

The secret of this trick is that the hole in the ball does not run straight through. It is actually two straight holes set at an angle to each other (see Figure 15).

When you hold the string tightly, friction between the ball and string prevents the ball from falling. When the string is relaxed, gravity takes over and the ball slides down the string.

FLYWHEEL TOYS

THE FRICTION-POWERED TRUCK

The friction-powered truck is really powered by your arm and hand. You run the wheels across the floor a few times and then let the truck go. It zooms along the floor under its own power.

When you drag the wheels across the floor, friction with the floor causes the wheels to spin. *A gear* on each axle of the wheels spins with them. These gears mesh as shown in Figure 16 with a series of gears that lead to a *flywheel*. The flywheel is a large disk spinning on the same axle as the final gear in the train. The gears are designed to get the flywheel spinning faster than the wheels.

The flywheel stores the *energy* that you give the truck when you get the wheels spinning. The faster a flywheel spins, the more energy it has. It transfers energy to the truck wheels, keeping them spinning after you stop pushing the truck along the floor.

FIGURE 16

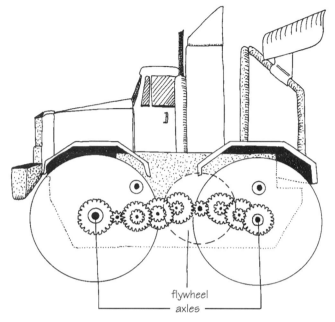

flywheel
axles

When you place the truck on the floor, the wheels need energy to continue spinning. They must now over-come friction with the floor and the *inertia* of the truck. Inertia is responsible for the tendency of objects to stay at rest when they're at rest (see p. 82). The flywheel supplies the necessary energy but slows down as it loses energy. When the energy is depleted, the truck comes to a stop.

Flywheels store energy so well because they have a lot of *rotational inertia*. Rotational inertia is the tendency of wheels to keep spinning once they're spinning. An opposing force, such as friction, however, can overcome this inertia and slow down a flywheel.

The rotational inertia of a flywheel is calculated by multiplying the mass of each of its sections by the square

FIGURE 17

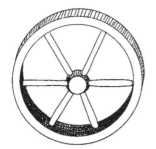

of its distance from the axle, and then adding the results. To increase a flywheel's rotational inertia, designers increase the amount of mass at the rim. An example of this kind of design is shown in Figure 17.

THE FRICTION-POWERED PLANE

The friction-powered plane works similarly to the friction-powered truck. You force the wheels along the floor, overcoming inertia, to get a flywheel spinning. The spinning flywheel then powers the plane along the floor.

The gear arrangement in the plane is much simpler than the truck's (see Figure 18). That's because the plane's flywheel does not have to store as much energy as the truck's flywheel. The plane weighs less than the truck because it has less mass, so there is less inertia to overcome.

As the wheels spin, a gear attached to the horizontal axle between the wheels spins with them. This gear is called a crown gear because it is shaped like a crown. Its teeth—the points of the crown—mesh with a small gear spinning on a vertical axle. Crown gears are designed to mesh with gears that are not on a parallel axle.

The flywheel is attached to the vertical axle of the small gear. Because the crown gear has a larger diameter than the other gear, the vertical axle spins faster than the horizontal axle between the wheels.

The large rotational inertia of the flywheel keeps the

41

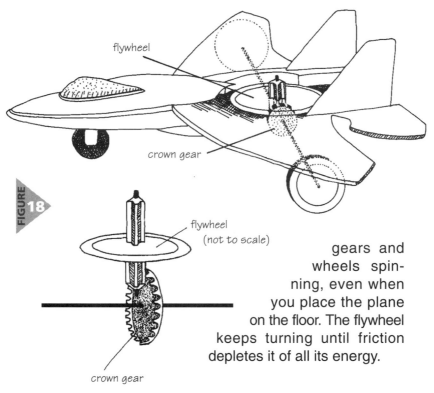

FIGURE 18

flywheel

crown gear

flywheel
(not to scale)

crown gear

gears and wheels spinning, even when you place the plane on the floor. The flywheel keeps turning until friction depletes it of all its energy.

THE WHIRLING BUTTON

The whirling button is so old that its beginnings are unknown. Fortunately for us, that makes the toy quite easy to make.

Find a large button and some strong string, and you're halfway to making this toy. The button should be about 2 in (5 cm) in diameter. Thread the string through the button as shown in Figure 19 and form a loop about 15 in (38 cm) long.

Place one finger of each hand in either end of the loop and twirl the button so that the string twists. After the string has twisted, jerk both fingers away from the button and then hold them still. The string will unwind and then wind itself up in the opposite direction.

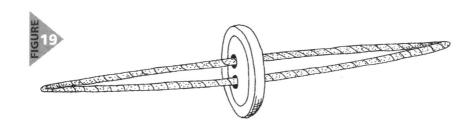

FIGURE 19

Once you get the rhythm of the motion, you can keep it up for some time. This toy may not sound like much fun when you read about it, but when you play with it, you'll find it almost hypnotic and difficult to put down.

The button acts as a flywheel. But in this toy, it stores its spinning energy in the string by twisting it. When the string is winding up, it is storing *potential energy,* energy that can be converted to motion at some time in the future. When you jerk on the string, the potential energy is converted to motion, or, to be precise, *kinetic energy*: that is, the button spins in the other direction.

Once the string has unwound, the button continues spinning, and the kinetic energy begins changing back into potential energy.

THE BUZZ SAW

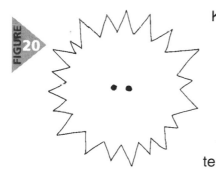

FIGURE 20

Kids sometimes make a variation on the whirling button. They cut a large circle out of heavy cardboard, making teeth at the circle's edge as shown in Figure 20. Then they thread string through two holes in the center as in the button version.

Next they place a piece of

paper so it hangs slightly off the edge of a table. Once they get the buzz saw spinning, they lightly touch the teeth to the paper's edge. This makes a sound just like a buzz saw cutting wood. See Chapter 5, on vibration toys, to find out why.

THE GYROSCOPE

The gyroscope is a toy you'll have to go out and buy. If you've never played with one before, you will be amazed.

Every time I pick up one of these and start to play with it, I am amazed all over again. I know how it works and why it works, but it's so cool to see it and feel it happening in my own hands.

The gyroscope is a flywheel spinning on an axle inside a cage (see Figure 21). To start the wheel spinning, you first must wind a string around the axle. Next, you hold onto the cage as you pull the string. This should get the wheel spinning rapidly.

Look at the point where the axle fits into the tiny

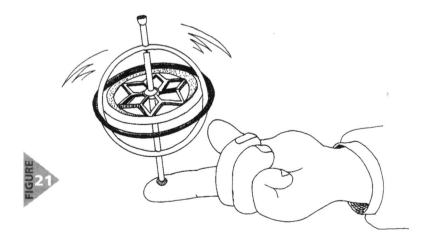

FIGURE 21

holes in the cage. Notice how smooth the ends of the wheel's axle are. The ends are polished so there will be as little friction as possible between the cage and the axle.

If there is too much friction, the wheel will not spin for long. You should also be aware that as the wheel spins, friction with the air helps slow it down.

Once you get the wheel spinning you can do some pretty amazing things. Here's a simple experiment:

Try to balance the gyroscope on one finger with the wheel spinning. Now try to balance it when the wheel is still. Why do you think it's easier to balance the gyroscope while the wheel is spinning?

It's because of the "gyroscopic effect." But what does that mean?

It has to do with the rotational inertia of the flywheel. As explained on p. 40, the inertia keeps the flywheel spinning unless it is opposed by a force such as friction. Rotational inertia also tends to keep the wheel spinning in the same plane. You can see this clearly by holding a spinning gyroscope by the cage and trying to twist the gyroscope out of position as in Figure 22a. You will feel the rotational inertia of the spinning wheel fighting you.

FIGURE 22

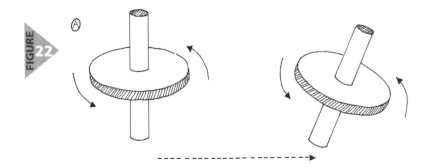
Ⓐ

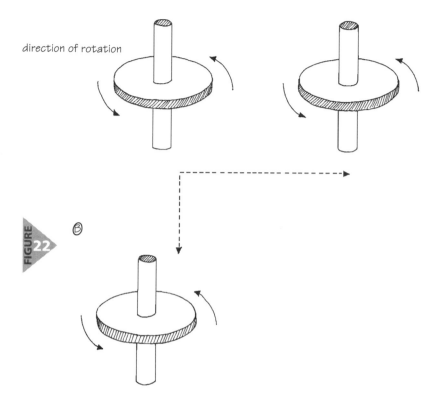

direction of rotation

FIGURE 22

Ⓑ

Now try moving a spinning gyroscope sideways while keeping the wheel in the same plane. What happens? When you don't try to twist the gyroscope, it moves easily. You can also move it easily when you move the gyroscope up and down, keeping the wheel parallel to its original position (see Figure 22b).

In his book *Thinking Physics*, Lewis Carroll Epstein offers a good way to visualize rotational inertia. It may help you understand it better.

Instead of a solid wheel, imagine a doughnut-shaped tube filled with water (see Figure 23a). The water is rushing around inside the tube in one direction. Now imagine that the doughnut is stretched into a square doughnut, with the water still rushing through it.

Imagine that the square doughnut is in position A, shown in Figure 23b. If we try to move the doughnut to position B, the rushing water will push against the side of the tube. This pushing force tends to prevent the doughnut from turning.

The result is the same with a gyroscope. As you try to turn it, the inertia of the spinning wheel fights your efforts. Like all flywheels, the one inside the gyroscope

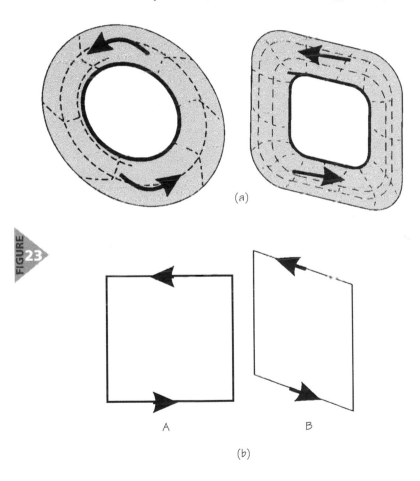

(a)

FIGURE 23

A   B

(b)

is thin at the center and thick toward its rim to maximize rotational inertia. To be most effective at staying upright, a gyroscope must have the majority of its mass as far from the center axle as possible.

THE YO-YO

The yo-yo is a simple toy with a long history. Illustrations of the yo-yo have been found on ancient Greek pottery dating back to 450 B.C., and French aristocrats played with what they called the *joujou de Normandie* in the 1790s.

When I was a kid, the "yo-yo man" used to come to our school every year in the spring-time. He would do the most incredible tricks with his yo-yo, explaining them as he went along. All of us kids would go out and buy one and learn how to do a couple of the tricks. Some of the easiest were walk the dog, the baby in the cradle, and around the world.

The Duncan Yo-Yo Company started making this toy in 1930. It makes what is probably the finest mass-produced yo-yo on the market today.

The yo-yo is a type of gyroscope. It consists of two round disks joined by an axle at their centers. A string is attached loosely to the axle as shown in Figure 24a. To begin playing with it, the string must be wound around the axle as in Figure 24b. It is highly recommended that you play with the yo-yo only outdoors and away from other people. Otherwise, you might hit someone.

FIGURE 24

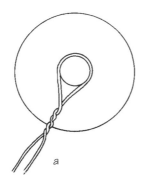
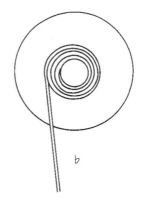

a   b

After looping the end of the string around your finger, throw the yo-yo toward the ground, and the string starts to unwind. As the string unwinds, the yo-yo spins around its axle. Because it is basically a gyroscope, the yo-yo tends to move straight up and down the string so that the spinning disks stay in the same plane.

At the start, when you wind the string on the axle, you are storing potential energy. As you let the yo-yo drop, the potential energy changes to kinetic energy. The yo-yo spins with increasing speed until it reaches the end of the string, storing kinetic energy as a flywheel does.

What happens next depends upon your ability as a yo-yoer. If you hold your hand still, the yo-yo usually rolls right back up the string. It rewinds the string around the axle as it goes, converting kinetic energy back into potential energy.

With some practice, you can get the yo-yo to sleep at the end of the string. That means the yo-yo spins in place; this is made possible by the loose attachment of the string to the axle. Try to get the yo-yo to sleep for 5 or 6 seconds and then, with just a flick of your wrist, climb back up the string. When you flick the wrist, the string loops around and binds to the axle. The flick also imparts some extra energy to the system, which helps the yo-yo return to your hand.

Once you get the knack of "sleeping," you can move on to more difficult moves like walking the dog, baby in the cradle, and around the world.

THE ELECTRIC YO-YO

The electric yo-yo works in much the same way as the regular one, but with an added feature. There is an electric circuit built into each disk. The circuit includes a switch, a battery, and a small light bulb (see Figure 25). As the yo-yo spins, the arm of the switch moves outward and closes the circuit, allowing electricity from the battery to pass to the bulb and light it up.

The reason the switch moves outward has to do with inertia. Isaac Newton's first law of motion says that an object in motion will stay in motion in a straight line, unless acted upon by an outside force (see p. 82). To understand this, imagine that you are twirling over your head a string with a rock tied to the end of it (see Figure 26). Would you feel the string tugging on your hand as the rock goes around?

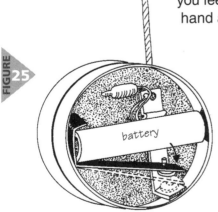

FIGURE 25

battery

The rock on the string is actually traveling in a straight line at each moment. Its inertia fights to keep it going straight, Newton says, but the force of the string on the rock pulls it into the circle. You are applying what is known as *centripetal*

FIGURE 26

force. In a flywheel or gear, the strength of its material prevents it from breaking apart and flying off; the structure of the material itself is exerting centripetal force.

But in this yo-yo, one end of the arm of the switch has no force pulling it toward the center of the yo-yo. So when the yo-yo spins, the arm flies outward until it is stopped by the electrical contact. When the yo-yo stops, a small spring returns the arm to its original position.

A common error people make is to call the tendency of objects to fly out of rotation, centrifugal force. The term implies that an outward force develops as a result of the rotating action, when in reality, the outward motion comes from the object's inertia.

THE BURP GUN

In World War II, GIs began calling machine guns burp guns because of the noise they make. This toy helps you pretend you're a soldier by mimicking the ratatat-ratatat sound of a machine gun. You'd be surprised how complicated the machinery must be to produce this simple sound.

The gun's trigger is the beginning of a gear train. The trigger itself is really a lever that has teeth on the

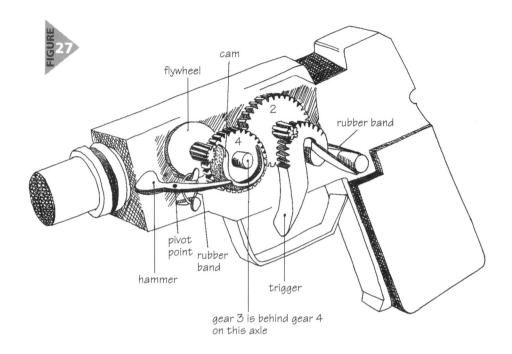

FIGURE 27

cam

flywheel

2

rubber band

4

rubber band

pivot
point

hammer

trigger

gear 3 is behind gear 4
on this axle

end inside the gun (see Figure 27). The teeth mesh with
a small gear (gear 1), so that when the trigger is pulled,
the small gear turns. The axle of the small gear is shared
by a larger gear (gear 2). Consequently, when the small
gear turns, the larger gear does too. The large gear
meshes with a second small gear (gear 3), which in turn
shares its axle with another large gear (gear 4).

Gear 4 has a mechanism called a *cam* built into its
side. The surface of the cam has a shape designed to
raise and lower a lever arm every time gear 4 makes a
rotation. At the other end of the lever is a small hammer that hits against the side of the burp gun whenever
the lever is lowered. When it hits, the hammer makes
a single "tat" sound. The *vibration* caused by the hammer hitting the inside of the gun is transferred to the air.
When the vibrating air reaches our ears, we perceive it
as sound.

We actually hear a "ratatat-ratatat" sound because the hammer hits many times a minute. The gears keep spinning rapidly even after the trigger has been pulled, thanks to a flywheel. It is on the same axle as a small gear that meshes with gear 4, so the flywheel starts spinning when you pull the trigger. When the gear train begins to slow down, the spinning flywheel transfers its energy to gear 4, and the hammer continues hitting.

There are two elastic rubber band springs in the gun. The first one returns the trigger to its starting position after it has been pulled. The second one pushes the hammer end of the lever against the side of the burp gun. After the cam moves the hammer end of the lever away from the gun, the rubber band slams it back into the gun's side to make the noise.

Remember to tell Mom that making noise with this toy is really a science experiment.

THE WHIRLING TOY

The whirling toy appears around holidays in many different designs. The version I will describe has a rotating

Christmas tree. To get the tree rotating, you must pump a plunger in and out.

As you pump the plunger, the tree spins faster and faster. Eventually, the tree opens up, like a four-sided clamshell, revealing a Santa figure. When you stop pushing the plunger, the tree slows and closes up, finally coming to a stop.

If you stop to analyze what is happening, you may be surprised. The way it works is truly fascinating.

As you push the plunger in, a series of actions happen. Inside the mechanism, the plunger has teeth that engage, or mesh with, gear 1 (see Figure 28). Gear 1 changes the straight-line motion of the plunger into rotary motion. The diameter of the gear is small so that small movements of the plunger translate to as much rotation as possible.

Because gear 1 is attached to spindle A, the spindle spins with gear 1. Gear 2 is also attached to spindle A, so it spins at the same number of revolutions per minute (rpms) as gear 1. Note that gear 1 is smaller in diameter than gear 2. Consequently, the circumference, or outer

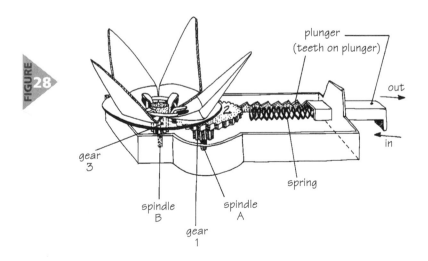

edge, of gear 2 always moves faster than the circumference of gear 1.

Gear 2 engages gear 3, which is on spindle B with Santa and the Christmas tree. Gear 3 is much smaller than gear 2, so the high speed at the circumference of gear 2 makes gear 3 spin very rapidly. Thus, spindle B rotates at higher revolutions per minute (rpms) than spindle A. In my model, Santa spins four times for every revolution of gear 1. That allows me to get Santa and the tree moving very rapidly with just a couple of pushes of the plunger.

An ingenious feature of the mechanism keeps Santa spinning even when you pull back on the plunger. Spindle A is free to move a bit in the direction of motion of the plunger. When the plunger goes in, its teeth push spindle A toward spindle B so that gear 2 meshes with gear 3. When you pull the plunger back, gear 2 disengages from gear 3. If it didn't disengage, gear 2, now turning in the opposite direction, would impede the spinning of Santa.

There is also a spring inside the mechanism that stretches as you push the plunger in. As you apply force to the spring, you are storing potential energy in it. When you stop pushing on the plunger, the spring relaxes back to its original shape, pulling the plunger back out of the mechanism. In the process, the potential energy in the spring is converted to kinetic energy. This motion quickly sets up the plunger for another push into the mechanism and makes sure gear 2 disengages quickly from gear 3.

When the tree is spinning rapidly enough, inertia (often mistakenly called centrifugal force) takes over. The tree tries to move away from the center of the retaining disk (see Figure 29). The tree retaining hooks act as pivots; the treetop rotates around the pivot away from the center. The tree sections soon open up completely until they are flattened against the retaining disk. The plastic Santa is now visible.

The four sections of the tree are revolving so rapidly that they become a transparent blur. Our eyes can't pick out the individual sections.

When you stop pushing on the plunger, you stop putting energy into the system. Rotational inertia keeps Santa going a while longer, but then friction overcomes it, and the system slows down.

As the tree opens, the rubber band holding the tree retaining hooks in place is stretched; potential energy is stored in the rubber band. As Santa slows down, the rubber band resumes its original shape, and this energy is converted to kinetic energy. The band pulls the hooks back in toward center, and the tree sections fold back up over Santa.

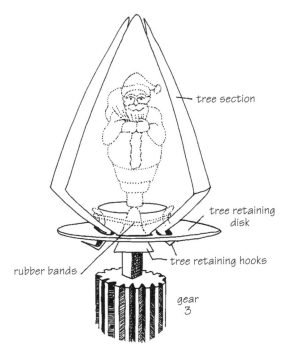

tree section

tree retaining disk

tree retaining hooks

rubber bands

gear 3

VIBRATION
TOYS

SNAKE EGGS

Here's another toy that's really a wonderful practical joke. You can make your friends jump with this one.

The idea is to hand an unsuspecting victim an envelope marked "SNAKE EGGS—HANDLE WITH CARE—DANGEROUS." You say, "Take a look at these. They're really cool."

As your friend opens the envelope, a vibration and a rattling noise emanate from inside. With the envelope's  warning in mind, the friend can't help but think that eggs have hatched into a real live snake! This gag has been known to make strong people scream and weak people run away.

Here's how to make one. Using pliers, bend about 6 in

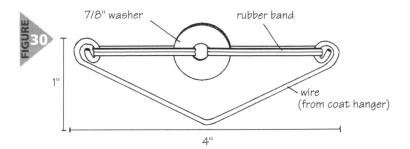

FIGURE 30

7/8" washer   rubber band

1"

wire
(from coat hanger)

4"

(15 cm) of wire from a coat hanger into the shape in Figure 30. Get a metal washer 7/8 in (2.2 cm) in diameter. Then thread a rubber band through the washer and attach it as shown to the loop at one end of the wire. Thread another rubber band through the washer and attach it to the other end.

Now rotate the washer 20 to 30 times so that you wind up the rubber bands. Making sure the rubber bands don't unwind, place the entire contraption in a small envelope about 1 1/2 in by 5 in (4 cm by 13 cm). Close the envelope by slipping the flap inside.

When your friend opens the envelope, the washer starts spinning. It hits against the side of the envelope, causing it to vibrate. The air around the envelope vibrates, too, and the vibrations are carried to your ears and your friend's ears as *sound* waves.

Close flap...but DON'T GLUE it down!

open with caution

When you wind the washer, you are storing a fair amount of potential energy in the rubber band by twisting it. When the envelope opens, the bands are able to untwist and the potential energy changes to kinetic energy: the washer rotates.

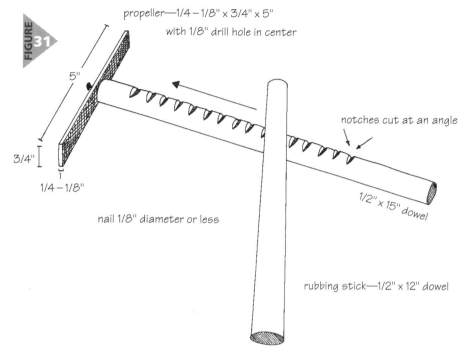

FIGURE 31

propeller—1/4 – 1/8" x 3/4" x 5"
with 1/8" drill hole in center

5"

3/4"

1/4 – 1/8"

nail 1/8" diameter or less

notches cut at an angle

1/2" x 15" dowel

rubbing stick—1/2" x 12" dowel

THE GEEHAW THINGAMAJIG

The geehaw thingamajig is an old-timer that has been around for well over a century and is still fun to play with. When you know the secret, you can get a "propeller" spinning on the end of a stick and then change the direction of its spin, as if by magic. If you don't know the secret, it can drive you nuts.

To put a geehaw thingamajig together, use Figure 31 as a guide. To make the propeller, drill an 1/8-in (3.2-mm)-diameter hole in the center of the wood stick. Drill a 3/32-in (2.4-mm)-diameter hole in the center of one end of the 15-in (38-cm) dowel. Then, with a saw, cut eight or so notches along one side of the dowel, starting about 2 in (5 cm) from the drilled end. The notches should be about 1/2 in (1 cm) apart.

FIGURE 32

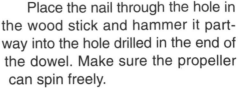

Place the nail through the hole in the wood stick and hammer it partway into the hole drilled in the end of the dowel. Make sure the propeller can spin freely.

Once you have a dowel to use as the rubbing stick, you are ready to operate the toy. Hold the rubbing stick tightly in your right hand and the notched dowel tightly in the left hand with the notches facing upward.

The idea is to rub back and forth vigorously on the notches as shown in Figure 32. If you don't know the secret, all you get is a bunch of noise. The noise comes from the vibrations set up by the stick hitting the notches. The vibrations cause the air to vibrate and to carry sound to our ears.

To learn the secret, look at Figure 33a. Notice how the right index finger is resting over both sticks. Hold the notched stick tightly in the left hand and as you rub back and forth, pull the notched stick gently toward the right with your bent index finger. This will cause the propeller to spin in one direction.

To get the propeller to change direction, release the right index finger from the notched stick. Push against the right side of the notched stick with your right thumb as in Figure 33b. While still holding the notched stick firmly in the left hand, push it gently toward the left with the thumb. This will cause the propeller to slow down and then start spinning in the other direction.

When only the left hand touches the notched stick, The vibrations run up and down the stick. When the right finger or thumb adds pressure, the vibrations become somewhat circular. As a result of the circular vibrations,

FIGURE 33

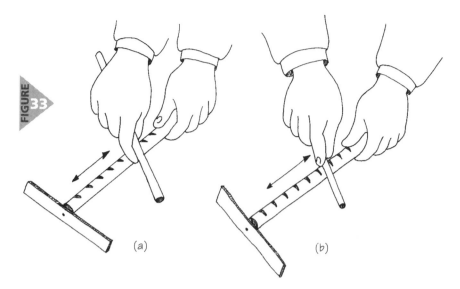

(a)   (b)

the nail also moves in a circular manner. The nail, moving in circles, drags the propeller with it. Even though the propeller is designed to spin freely on the nail, there is still some friction present. The propeller starts turning and will continue turning until the vibrations stop.

Depending upon the finger used—thumb or forefinger—and the direction pushed, the circular vibrations are either clockwise or counterclockwise. If you would like to see the vibrations a little more clearly, try mounting a tiny piece of plastic mirror on the head of the nail and shining a light on it.

When you make the propeller turn first in one direction and then the other, you can actually follow the path of the reflected light. See how the path changes when using no finger, one finger, and then the other.

THE BULL ROARER

The bull roarer is very simple to make, and can drive people crazy with the noise it generates.

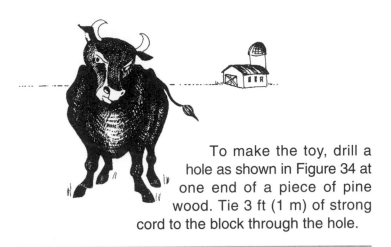

To make the toy, drill a hole as shown in Figure 34 at one end of a piece of pine wood. Tie 3 ft (1 m) of strong cord to the block through the hole.

To operate the toy, hold the free end of the cord and start to whirl the bull roarer around your head as in Figure 35. As soon as it gets spinning, you should hear a strange noise. Do you see now why the toy is called a bull roarer? You can vary the sound quality by varying the bull roarer's speed.

Where does the sound come from? As the bull roarer moves through the air, the block and the cord vibrate, setting up air vibrations. Because your bull roarer spins in a circle, the vibrations repeat at set intervals, resulting in a low-pitched moaning. If you speed up or slow down the rota-

34 FIGURE

1/4" x 2" x 8"
(0.6 cm x 5 cm x 20 cm)

FIGURE 35

tions, the interval between vibrations changes and the moaning has a slightly different pitch.

As you learned in the previous chapter, you are applying centripetal force to the cord to keep the block moving in a circle.

LEVER
TOYS

THE JUMPING JACK

The Jumping Jack can be found in many toy shops but can just as easily be made at home. If you buy one, you'll probably find it's made of wood or plastic, but you can make one out of cardboard.

The easiest way to make this toy is to reproduce Figure 36 on a copying machine. Do not rip the page out of the book because you will lose the information on the other side of the page.

With rubber cement or glue, attach the reproduction to a piece of cardboard. When the glue has dried, carefully cut out Jack's body parts with scissors. Pierce a hole at the black dots with a carpenter's nail, and pierce the x's with a straight pin. Attach each arm and leg to the body by inserting a brass paper fastener (you can get them at stationery stores) through the large holes. The arms and legs should move freely around the fasteners.

Turn Jack facedown and rotate his arms and legs

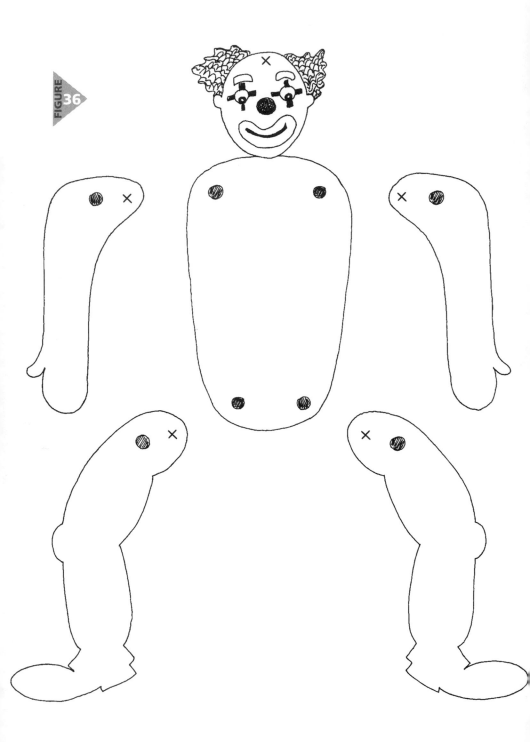

FIGURE 36

FIGURE 37

back
view

downward. Connect the arms by threading a short piece of thin string through the holes at the *x*'s (see Figure 45). Connect the legs in the same way. The strings between the arms and legs should not sag.

Attach a loop of string through the hole in the top of the head. With another piece of string, tie the arm and leg strings together, allowing about 12 in (30 cm) of string to hang from the bottom of Jack.

If you wish, you may now decorate the Jumping Jack to your heart's content with crayons, paint, or colored pencils.

To see Jack in action, attach the loop at his head to the wall with a thumbtack and allow him to hang. Now gently pull the string hanging from his body. The arms and legs should fly up in the air as in Figure 38. When you release the string, the arms and legs should return to their original position.

This simple toy illustrates one of the most basic elements of machines: levers (see p. 84). Jack's arms and legs act as levers. A lever is a bar that rotates about a pivot point called a *fulcrum*. In this case, the brass paper fasteners act as fulcrums.

You apply force at the point where the string attaches to each appendage; you pull down on the string, and the tops of the arms and legs move downward. The arms and legs rotate around their respective

fulcrums—the paper fasteners—and the out-put force lifts the arms and legs in the air.

This lever arrangement changes the straight-line motion of the string into circu-lar motion. More importantly, it multiplies the small movement of the applied force to create a large movement of the hands and feet. You may move the string only 1/2 in (1 cm), but the arms and legs may move about 3 in (8 cm).

If you'd like to try another design, copy the elephant parts in Figure 40, and use Figure 39 as a guide in assembling it. Then use your imagination to come up with your own design. You could decorate a whole room with these toys!

FIGURE 39

front

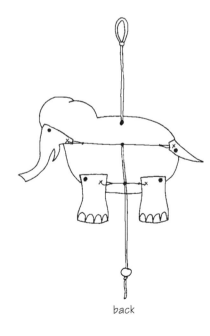

back

FIGURE 40

SPRING-POWERED
TOYS

BOW AND ARROW

The bow and arrow are great fun to play with. Except for the suction cup on the end of the arrow, the toy in Figure 41 works just like a real bow and arrow, which has been used as a weapon and for hunting for thousands of years. According to an article in the June 1991 *Scientific American,* scientists have found bows dating to as early as 6000 B.C.!

The bow and string act as a spring. When you pull back the string, you are storing potential energy in the spring. When your fingers release the arrow and the string, the potential energy is converted to kinetic energy and the arrow speeds toward (we hope) the target. For an explanation of how the suction cup tip works, see page 18.

NOTE *Do not point or shoot an arrow at people or animals; you could injure them.*

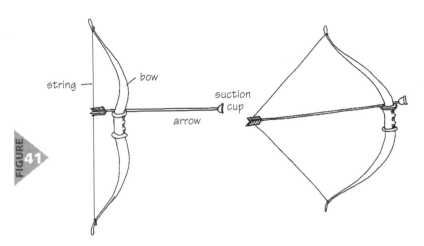

FIGURE 41

string —

bow

suction cup

arrow

THE SPRING-POWERED DART GUN

The spring-powered dart gun may be difficult to find in some areas because the hard plastic darts can cause injuries if they are not used properly. If you have one, *make sure you never point the gun at anyone, even when it is not loaded.*

This gun offers a good example of how springs work. To load the gun, you simply push a dart down the center of the barrel. When it locks in place, you're ready to test your aim. The dart sticks to your target (if it's a nonporous surface) because of the suction cup on the end.

The mechanism inside the gun is surprisingly simple. The whole toy has only three moving parts: the dart, the trigger, and the coil spring (see Figure 42).

At the back of the dart is a small ledge that, during loading, moves over the lip at the top end of the trigger. The lip slips under the ledge and locks the dart in place, even as the spring begins pushing forward on the dart. The locking is aided by the lip's upward push, which comes from the force of the spring on the back of the trigger near its pivot point. The trigger acts as a lever (see p. 84).

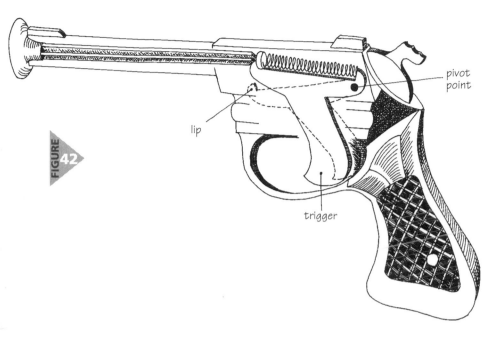

pivot
point

lip

trigger

When you pull back on the trigger, the force you apply is transferred to the lip, pulling it down. Now the potential energy stored in the compressed spring is converted to kinetic energy. The spring expands and pushes the dart out the gun.

WINDUP
TOYS

WALKING DINOSAUR

Windup toys come in many shapes. One of the most popular right now is the walking dinosaur. It has some operating features that are quite ingenious.

Most windup toys have at their heart a watchwork motor, which as you may have guessed is similar to the mechanism found in windup watches. All watchwork motors have a handle or key like the one in Figure 43 to wind a spring.

The spring is a coil of flat wire that winds tightly as you turn the key. The key is attached to the inner end of the coil, and the outer end is held stationary by its connection to the motor case. As you wind the toy, you are storing potential energy in the spring.

The key is also attached through an axle to a *ratchet gear*. Situated inside the main gear, the ratchet gear meshes with the inner diameter of the main gear. The teeth on these two gears are designed to allow the ratchet gear to engage with the main gear only when

FIGURE 43

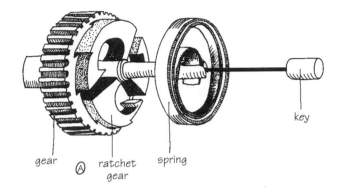

key

gear Ⓐ ratchet spring
gear

it's turning in one direction (counterclockwise in Figure 43). When you wind the spring clockwise, the ratchet gear's teeth slip past the main gear's teeth. When you stop winding, the tension in the spring locks the teeth of the ratchet gear back against the teeth of the main gear, concentrating all the potential energy on the main gear.

The spring will not unwind unless the toy is free to move. When you set the toy on the ground, the ratchet and main gear turn as one unit powered by the spring. The teeth on the outside of the main gear mesh with a smaller gear as shown in Figure 44. Attached to the axle of the smaller gear is the power take-off gear. It is connected through a shaft to a pair of cams that move the dinosaur's legs. The stabilizer gear keeps the power take-off gear balanced on its axle.

Notice that the main gear turns at fewer rpms than the final output gear. That means for every full revolution the main gear turns, the output gear may turn five times or more.

Each cam rotates inside a hole in a flat plate on either side of the dinosaur. As the cams turn, they push one plate back and the other one forward. Each flat plate is connected to one front and one back leg. The legs act as levers; when a plate moves forward, it

FIGURE 44

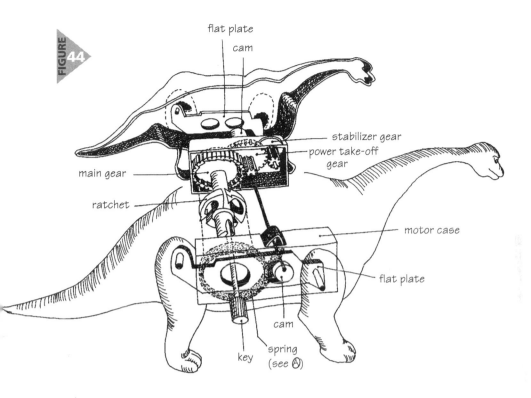

flat plate

cam

stabilizer gear

power take-off gear

main gear

ratchet

motor case

flat plate

cam

key

spring (see Ⓐ)

pushes the front leg around its pivot point, moving the leg forward and upward off the walking surface. At the same time, the rear leg pivots down and backward onto the walking surface.

Just the opposite happens on the other side. The front leg rotates down onto the surface and to the back, and the rear leg rotates forward and upward off the surface. The legs move back and forth with each rotation of the cam and the dinosaur moves forward.

The dinosaur would not be able to walk if its weight were not distributed correctly. It is designed so that its weight shifts to whichever legs are moving to the rear, because those are the two legs that are touching the walking surface and moving the dinosaur forward.

REVIEW OF SCIENTIFIC PRINCIPLES

MATTER AND ENERGY

Everything around us is made of matter. Things made of matter include trees, cars, dogs, cats, mice, broccoli, water, ice cream, TV sets, bicycles, teachers, cockroaches, and rosebushes.

Matter is made up of atoms. There are 92 naturally occurring atoms on the earth. When atoms exist individually or combine with identical atoms, the end result is called an element. When atoms combine with dissimilar atoms, the end result is called a compound. There are thousands and thousands of compounds on the earth.

The only stuff in the universe that is not made up of matter is energy, such as solar, electrical, or nuclear energy.

Neither matter nor energy can be created or destroyed, but energy can be converted into matter and matter can be converted into energy.

When a tree grows in the forest, it converts and stores energy from the sun, combining it with compounds and elements from the air and the forest floor. This process creates leaves, wood, and sap; energy is converted to matter.

We can use the stored energy by burning the wood. To withdraw the energy, we must change the form of the wood, converting some of it back into energy and the rest into ashes.

If we wish, we can withdraw the energy from radioactive substances slowly, carefully, and productively in a nuclear reactor. That energy can then be used in homes and factories across the land. There are many safe nuclear power generating plants across the United States and the rest of the world. But if we are not careful, we can end up with a nuclear disaster such as the incident at Three Mile Island in Pennsylvania or at Chernobyl in Russia.

If we release energy from radioactive substances violently, we end up with an atomic bomb like the one that destroyed Hiroshima, Japan.

MASS AND WEIGHT

Mass is a measure of the total amount of matter in an object. The weight of an object can also indicate how much matter it has, but there is a difference between mass and weight.

First, imagine a brick, much like the brick on the outside of a building. Next, imagine a sponge the same exact size and color as the brick.

If one of them had to drop on your toe from a height of 5 ft (1.5 m), and you had the choice of which one it would be, you'd probably pick the sponge, unless there were something seriously wrong with your brain and your name was Beavis.

That's because the brick weighs more than the sponge, even though they are the same size. The atoms that make up a brick are packed together more tightly than those in a sponge. In very simple terms, there is more stuff in a brick than in a sponge. The more matter an object has, the greater its mass.

Weight is a measurement of the pull of gravity on the mass of an object. If you weigh 125 pounds (57 kilograms) on earth, you would weigh approximately one-sixth that weight, or about 21 lbs (9.5 kg), on the moon. You would weigh nothing if you were floating around in space, where everything is in free fall. Although the pull of gravity may change, you still have the same mass. Weight is dependent on the pull of gravity. Mass remains the same regardless of gravity.

General Properties of Matter

▶ **Matter cannot be created.**

▶ **Matter cannot be destroyed.**

▶ **All matter takes up space.**

▶ **Matter exists in three states: solids, liquids, and gases.**

A solid has a definite volume and shape. Some examples of solids are baseball bats, baseballs, roller skates, frying pans, ice cream cones, and ice cubes.

A liquid has a definite volume but no definite shape. Examples of liquids are water, milk, gasoline, and chocolate syrup.

A gas has no definite shape and no definite volume. Examples of gases are the exhaust gases of a car, the air we breathe, the helium gas that fills a balloon, and steam rising from a boiling pan of water.

Most matter can exist in all three states. States

can change as a result of changes in pressure or temperature or a combination of both. For example, consider water at normal atmospheric pressure. At a temperature below 32° F (0° C), water exists as a solid that we know as ice. Between 32° F and 212° F (100° C), water is in its liquid state. Above 212° F, water is a gas. Increasing the pressure on water raises the temperatures at which water changes state.

▶ **All matter conforms to three laws of motion defined by Sir Isaac Newton in 1687.**

LAW 1

a. An object at rest will stay at rest unless acted upon by an outside force.
b. An object in motion will stay in motion in a straight line unless acted upon by an outside force.

LAW 2

An object acted upon by a constant force will accelerate constantly in the direction of the force.

LAW 3

For every action there is an equal and opposite reaction.

▶ **All matter exhibits inertia:**

LAW 1 is also known as the law of inertia. When something is moving, it will keep moving unless something stops it or makes it change direction. When an object is at rest, it will stay that way unless something moves it.

Say you were stranded in a spacesuit in outer space where there's no gravity or friction. If you kicked a rock, that rock would move away from you in a straight line. It would keep on going in a straight line for millions of miles until it hit a planet or star, entered the gravity field of a planet or star, or maybe was sideswiped by a meteor or comet. Only then would it slow down or change direction.

If you were to throw a ball in your schoolyard, there are a few reasons why it wouldn't go sailing off into space:

a. Friction between the atmosphere and ball slows the ball down.

b. Gravity pulls the ball down to the surface of the earth.

c. As the ball rolls across the playground, friction brings it to a stop.

If a ball were resting on a tabletop in your home, it would not move unless something moved it. That something could be you or a friend, a hurricane's winds, an earthquake, or maybe a truck crashing into the house.

▶ **Matter at a distance from an axis has rotational inertia about that axis.**

When an object spins about an axis, rotational inertia tends to keep the object spinning. Just as mass moving in a straight line resists a change in motion, mass moving in circles resists a change in rotational motion.

Rotational inertia is calculated by multiplying the mass of the object by the square of its distance from the axis. Thus, the greater the mass and the greater the distance from the axis, the greater the rotational inertia.

SIMPLE MACHINES

The Inclined Plane

An inclined plane is a flat surface that is set at an angle. For example, a plank going from the ground to the back of a truck is an inclined plane. It takes less force to push or pull an object up an inclined plane than it takes to lift it straight up. The price for this advantage is that the object must travel a greater distance when it goes up the incline. Other examples of inclined planes are ramps and stairs.

The Screw

A screw or bolt is an example of a specialized inclined plane. If the threads were "unrolled," they would form an incline. The incline makes it easier to push a wood screw into wood, for example. But instead of going straight in, the screw must be rotated a number of times to pay for the advantage.

The Lever

A lever is a bar that turns about a pivot point called a fulcrum. People use levers for several reasons: to make a small force larger, to make a small motion larger, or simply to move the location of a force.

If you apply a small force (the input force) at a large distance from the fulcrum, the lever can produce a large output force a short distance from the fulcrum. In Figure 45a, for example, the output force could lift a resistance, such as a large weight that you could not lift without the lever. The applied force multiplied by its distance from the fulcrum equals the output force multiplied by its distance from the fulcrum.

You can easily see this principle for yourself on a seesaw: The closer you move to the fulcrum of the seesaw, the harder it becomes to lift your friend on the other end. That's because the distance of the input force from the fulcrum is decreasing, reducing the amount of output force produced at the other end of the seesaw.

Levers are classified according to the location of the fulcrum in relation to the input and output forces. In first-

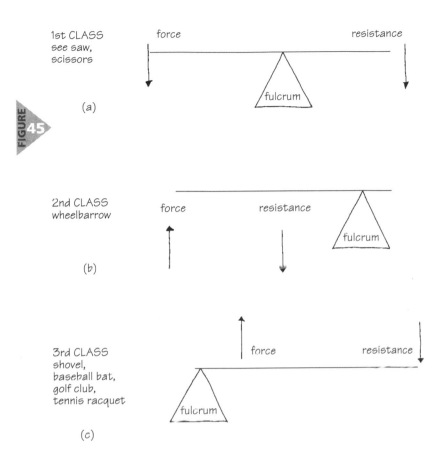

1st CLASS
see saw,
scissors

force

resistance

fulcrum

(a)

FIGURE 45

2nd CLASS
wheelbarrow

force

resistance

fulcrum

(b)

3rd CLASS
shovel,
baseball bat,
golf club,
tennis racquet

force

resistance

fulcrum

(c)

class levers, the fulcrum is between the input and output forces. First-class levers include scissors, pliers, claw hammers, and nail pullers. The fulcrum is on the end of second-class levers, with the output force in the middle (see Figure 45b). They include wheelbarrows and garlic presses. In third-class levers, the applied force is between the fulcrum and the output force (Figure 45c). Because the applied force is closer to the fulcrum, the output force is always smaller than the input force. These levers, which include hammers, tennis racquets, and baseball bats, are used when the goal is to multiply the movement or speed of the applied force. First-class levers can also be used for that purpose.

The Pulley

A simple pulley can be used to change the direction of applied force. A compound pulley, or block and tackle, can not only change the direction of the applied force but increase it. Once again, as in the inclined plane and the lever, the applied force must travel a greater distance to get the mechanical advantage than it otherwise would.

The Wheel and Axle

The wheel decreases friction by changing sliding motion to rolling motion. Because the wheel has a larger diameter than the axle, it also multiplies the input force on the axle.

The Gear

The gear is a special kind of wheel that transfers rotary motion to another rotating gear or linear mechanism. It has teeth on its outer diameter to prevent slippage between the two parts. The teeth on one part interlock with the teeth on the other: in other words, the two parts mesh. A gear can also drive a chain, such as a bicycle chain.

PRESSURE

Pressure is force applied over a surface area. When you press an elevator button, your finger puts pressure over the area you touch on the button. Gases and liquids exert pressure on the surfaces that contain them or any other surface they come into contact with. When you blow up a balloon, the air inside the balloon exerts pressure on the inner skin of the balloon. If you've had too many hot dogs and sodas and your stomach feels bloated and painful, you are experiencing gas pressure.

The pressure gases and liquids exert is determined by the forces on them and by their temperatures. As you go deeper into a lake, an ocean, or a swimming pool, water pressure increases because the weight of the water above you increases. Air pressure decreases the higher you go on a mountainside or in an airplane. Higher temperatures produce greater pressures as gases and liquids try to expand. Simply adding more gas or liquid to a confined space also increases the pressure.

GLOSSARY

air pressure—the amount of force per unit surface area that air exerts on anything it comes into contact with. Air pressure sometimes refers to atmospheric pressure.

atmospheric pressure—air pressure caused by the weight of the atmosphere. At sea level and 70° F, it is about 14.7 lbs per square inch (10.1 N/cm²). That means that for every square inch of surface area it touches, air is pushing down, up, or to the side with a force equal to 14.7 lbs of weight.

cam—a rotating mechanical part with a specially shaped surface. It is usually designed to create a repetitive motion in a second part that rests on its surface.

centripetal force—the force that produces circular motion by pulling a moving object toward the center of rotation.

elastic—returns to the original shape after being pushed, squeezed, or pulled. Springs and rubber bands are elastic.

energy—the work a system is capable of accomplishing.

flywheel—a wheel that stores mechanical energy by spinning. As a flywheel speeds up, it stores energy generated by a system, and as it slows down, it transfers energy back to the system. To be most effective in storing energy, a flywheel should have a greater amount of mass at the rim than at the hub: that is, it should have a lot of rotational inertia.

force—a push or a pull.

friction—a force that opposes the relative motion of two surfaces that are in contact with each other. Sometimes called drag, friction resists motion along the line of contact only. Air friction is the drag on objects that comes from a layer of air next to their surfaces.

gear—a wheel with teeth on its rim. These teeth mesh, or interlock, with teeth on other gears to transmit the force of one spinning gear to another with no slippage. To multiply the speed of a rotating shaft, a large diameter gear is added to the shaft. The rapidly moving teeth of the large gear mesh with a small diameter gear, which must make many revolutions for each revolution of the large gear. Therefore, the shaft of the small gear rotates much faster than the first shaft.

kinetic energy—energy of motion, exhibited by a body that is moving with some velocity. The object is actively accomplishing work rather than simply having the potential to do so. A flowerpot falling from a windowsill, for example, has kinetic energy. The kinetic energy comes from the conversion of potential energy stored when the pot was raised to the windowsill.

magnetic domain—the smallest region of uniform magnetization within a magnet. Although it is microscopic, it has a north pole and a south pole just as a magnet does. The magnetic domains, all taken together, are responsible for the magnetic field of a magnet.

magnetic induction—the process by which a magnetizable material, such as iron, becomes magnetized when a magnet is placed close to it.

mechanical advantage—the lessening of the force needed to accomplish work by some device such as a lever. The advantage must be paid for in some way: for example, the force may have to move a greater distance than it would without the advantage.

nonporous—does not allow the passage of gases or liquids; see *porous*.

O-ring—a rubber ring used to seal mechanical parts to prevent the leaking of a liquid or gas.

porous—having tiny holes or pores that allow the passage of gases or liquids.

potential energy—energy an object possesses because of its position. When released from the position, the object can accomplish work. A flowerpot on a windowsill, for example, has potential energy; when released from the sill, the pot will fall to the floor and the potential energy will change to kinetic energy.

pressure—the amount of force per unit surface area.

ratchet gear—a gear with slanted teeth designed to engage when rotating in one direction only.

sound—vibrations created by matter and carried by the air to our ears. We hear the vibrations as sound.

valve—a mechanical device that opens and closes to control the flow of a liquid or gas.

vibration—a rapid, back-and-forth motion of matter.

work—accomplished when a force causes something to move.

FOR FURTHER READING

Blocksma, Mary. *Action Contraptions*. New York: Simon & Schuster, 1987.

Daiken, Leslie. *Children's Toys Through the Ages*. London: Spring Books, 1988.

Epstein, Lewis Carroll. *Thinking Physics*. San Francisco: Insight Press, 1978.

Hillier, Mary. *Automata and Mechanical Toys*. London: Bloomsbury Books, 1988.

Macauly, David. *The Way Things Work*. Boston: Houghton Mifflin, 1988.

Ritchie, Carson. *Making Scientific Toys*. Nashville: Thomas Nelson, 1976.

Walker, Jearl. *The Flying Circus of Physics*. New York: John Wiley & Sons, 1977.

INDEX

ABOUT THE AUTHOR

Bob Friedhoffer has a master's degree in liberal studies, with an emphasis on the history and philosophy of science, from the City University of New York. Also known as the Madman of Magic, he has been performing as a magician for almost thirty years for children and young adults all over the country. He frequently gives lectures on science and magic. His entertaining approach to learning about science can be found in many other books he has written for Franklin Watts. The Scientific Magic series contains six volumes on the physics principles involved in magic tricks. His books *Magic Tricks, Science Facts* and *More Magic Tricks, Science Facts* were named by *Science Books and Films* to the "Best Children's Science Book List" for 1990 and 1991, respectively. He lives in New York City with his wife, Annette.